W9-AZG-519

UNDERSTANDING RELIGIONS

HINDUISM

HINDUISM

VASUDHA NARAYANAN

ROSEN
PUBLISHING®

New York

This edition published in 2010 by:

The Rosen Publishing Group, Inc.
29 East 21st Street
New York, NY 10010

Additional end matter copyright © 2010 by The Rosen Publishing Group, Inc.

Cover design by Nelson Sá.

Library of Congress Cataloging-in-Publication Data

Narayanan, Vasudha.
Hinduism / Vasudha Narayanan.
     p. cm.—(Understanding religions)
Includes bibliographical references and index.
ISBN-13: 978-1-4358-5620-2 (library binding)
1. Hinduism—Juvenile literature. I. Title.
BL1203.N37 2009
294.5—dc22

                                                    2009011026

Manufactured in Malaysia

Copyright © Duncan Baird Publishers
Text copyright © Duncan Baird Publishers
Commissioned artwork copyright © Duncan Baird Publishers

CONTENTS

INTRODUCTION

Eighty percent of India's population of more than one billion people are Hindu, and there are Hindus living in every part of the world today. Yet the term "Hinduism" is somewhat difficult to define. The religion has no single founder, creed, teacher, or prophet acknowledged by all Hindus as central to the religion, and no single holy book is universally acclaimed as being of primary importance.

The use of the word "Hindu" is itself complex. Both "India" and "Hindu" derive from Sindhu, the traditional name of the Indus River. In ancient inscriptions and documents, "Hindu" refers to the people of "Hind," the Indian subcontinent. In the Muslim-ruled empires of medieval India, it was used for many non-Muslim Indian communities. Although the term is found in Hindu literature earlier, it was only after the late eighteenth century that it became popular as a name for the dominant religion of the Indian people.

Hindus ordinarily identify themselves with reference to their caste, community, region, and language. The phrase *sanatana dharma* ("eternal faith") has become popular in the last two centuries, but it applies more to philosophical interpretations of the religion than to its colorful local manifestations. In early texts, *sanatana dharma* meant the ideal religious obligations of human beings, but it did not express the idea of a community of faith.

In Indian law, the term "Hindu" may even include those who belong to traditions usually thought of as theologically distinct from Hinduism. It is generally applied to anyone who lives in India and accepts the Hindu tradition—which is not defined—in any of its forms or developments. This therefore embraces Buddhists, Jains, and Sikhs. The term also applies to anyone else who is not a Muslim, Christian, Parsi (Zoroastrian), or Jew.

On the other hand, "Hinduism" has been a problematic label even for some traditions that many people would generally consider to be Hindu. At different times several Indian sects and movements have gone to court to argue against their official "Hindu" status.

Hinduism has been portrayed in the last two centuries as being a more or less unified religion. However, it is important to note that there are hundreds of internal divisions created by caste, community, language, and geography. Regional manifestations of a deity or a local sacred text may sometimes be more significant to a particular group of worshippers than any pan-Hindu concept. Many such groups may extensively share

Early morning bathing at the Shivsagar tank during the
Shivaratri Festival. The tank is the most famous feature
in the city of Shivsagar, which means "the ocean of Shiva."

common texts, deities, traditions, and patterns of
ritual, even though they interpret them variously; but
there may be other groups with whom they have very
little in common. Yet there are also threads that run
geographically throughout the subcontinent and histor-
ically across thousands of years. At certain times,
therefore, it may be more useful to talk of many Hindu
traditions, and at others, of one tradition.

Is Hinduism a religion, a culture or, as many Hindus

would say, a way of life? It is all three, but what in the West might be viewed as the boundaries between the sacred and nonsacred spheres do not apply to the Hindu traditions. While many Hindu holy texts and practices are intended to provide the devotee with spiritual paths to liberation from the repeated cycle of life and death, many other aspects of Hindu life and ritual do not lead directly to such transformation, but are perceived to enhance one's quality of life on earth. Thus such activities as tree-planting, singing, dancing, healing, archery, astrology, sculpture, architecture, and building a home might all be considered part of the religious domain.

In studying the many Hindu traditions, therefore, the words "secular" and "sacred" have to be used with caution. More meaningful terms in some Hindu contexts are *dharma* and *moksha*. *Dharma*, a Sanskrit word from a root meaning "to sustain," is truth, right-eousness, duty, law, and justice. *Moksha* literally means "liberation," that is, liberation from the cycle of life and death that every soul is believed to undergo (see pp. 90–95) and which is repeated endlessly, until such time as the soul achieves liberation into a state of bliss. While not unique to Hinduism, the belief in this process is perhaps one of the few concepts that most "Hindus" can be said to share.

CHAPTER ONE

ORIGINS AND HISTORICAL DEVELOPMENT

There is no specific year or even century for the beginnings of the Hindu tradition. It is a cumulative collection of communities, faiths, beliefs, and practices that have come together over the centuries, although its ancient roots are traditionally seen in the cultures of the Indus Valley, Saraswati River civilization, and Indo-European people. Sophisticated philosophies, village deities, and ethical obligations have all coexisted in pluralistic Hindu societies. Local traditions have entered Hinduism through processes of "Sanskritization," whereby a regional deity becomes identified with pan-Indian gods, and "brahminization," the adoption of "high"-caste rituals by many communities. While India is the *locus classicus* of the tradition, it has flourished in southeast Asia for more than fifteen hundred years, and now, in every part of the world.

LEFT: A woman pilgrim at Varanasi, the city on the Ganges that has for centuries been considered one of the most sacred places in Hinduism— a heavenly prototype.

The Hindu tradition has no founder figure and cannot date its origin to a particular year or century. It is generally believed that its beginnings lie in the ancient indigenous culture of India and of the Indo-European people. It is a matter of scholarly and political controversy whether the Indo-European people were the indigenous inhabitants of India or whether they migrated from outside. The stages of early Hindu history are marked not by remarkable personalities (although there have been many) and great proselytizing movements, but rather by the composition of philosophically sophisticated, edifying, or entertaining texts that were transmitted orally and through the generations primarily by means of the performing arts.

The earliest known Indian civilization existed ca. 3000–1750 BCE in a broad area around the region of the Indus river and other parts of India. Entire cities have been excavated, for example, at Harappa and Mohenjo Daro. The people of this civilization (often referred to as Harappan) were literate, but their script remains undeciphered. Some Harappan seals bear images of figures that share characteristics with the later Hindu deity Shiva. The huge pool complex at Mohenjo Daro known as the "Great Bath" may have possessed a religious function. From such fragmentary evidence we can tentatively state that some features of the present-day Hindu religion may be nearly five thousand years old.

The Indo-Europeans referred to themselves as "Aryans" or "Noble Ones." Their speech was the ancestor of the ancient Indian language of Sanskrit, which is closely related to all the other tongues referred to by linguists as "Indo-European," including Latin, Greek, and English. The earliest compositions in the Hindu tradition are the *Veda*s (Sanskrit, "Knowledge"), which form the core of India's ancient "proto-Hindu" religion and constitute manuals of poetry, rituals, and philosophy. A dominant feature of religious life in the Vedic period was ritual sacrifice. Most rituals involved fire and were conducted by ritual specialists and priests who also supervised the making of altars, utilizing precise mathematical measurements, and the recitation of hymns. Many sacrifices involved the use of *soma*, an intoxicating liquid.

Vedic religion perceived a delicate connection between the performance of rituals and the prevalence of *rta* ("truth," "justice," and "rightness"). *Rta* makes harmony and peace possible on earth and in the heavens and was upheld by early Vedic gods, such as Varuna. According to Vedic hymns, the world itself may have come into being through an act of cosmic sacrifice. One creation hymn explicitly mentions the beginnings of the social divisions that are referred to today as "caste" (see pp. 98–103).

The sacrifice-based worldview of the early Vedic age gave way to philosophical inquiry and discussion in the later texts known as the *Aranyaka*s and *Upanishad*s (see pp. 38–45). These were composed around the early sixth century BCE, a time of great intellectual speculation, when many religious leaders questioned and even rejected the authoritarian structures of traditional Indian religion, such as the religious leadership of the priestly caste (the *brahmin*s), the caste system itself, and the status of the *Veda*s.

The sophisticated philosophy of the *Upanishad*s was contemporaneous with the spirit of critical inquiry in many parts of northern India. Siddhartha Gautama (the Buddha) and Mahavira the Jina ("Victorious One," whose followers are today's Jains) both challenged the notion that the *Veda*s were divine revelation. Siddhartha and Mahavira emphasized nonviolence (*ahimsa*), and this virtue has also been very significant in Hinduism. In modern times, it informed the strategy of Mohandas Karamchand Gandhi (known as the Mahatma or "Great Soul"), who led India's struggle for independence in the twentieth century.

The *Upanishad*s sought liberation from the cycle of life and death and introduced the notion of immortality as reality. The ultimate quest of the Hindu tradition, as it subsequently developed, has been to achieve the immortality of the soul and, in this life, happiness and peace. The restless quest of these texts is seen in a line in the *Mundaka Upanishad*: "What is it that being known, all else becomes known?"

Most of the later literature in Sanskrit deals directly or indirectly with *dharma* (a word with multiple layers of meaning, including "righteous behavior," "truth," and "law"). These concepts are embedded in epic narratives called the *Ramayana* and the *Mahabharata*. The epics portray deeds of the incarnations of the deity Vishnu who is one of the prominent gods in Hinduism. The *Bhagavad Gita* ("Sacred Song") is eighteen chapters in the *Mahabharata* and emphasizes that *dharma* should be performed without expectation of reward but with devotion to one God. The "supreme being," conceived of in the *Upanishad*s as *brahman*, an abstract concept (see p. 25), is referred to in the *Bhagavad Gita* as the deity Krishna or Vishnu. Devotionalism (*bhakti*)—the intensely personal worship of, and surrender to, this supreme being, whether it be manifest in the form of Vishnu, Shiva, the Goddess, or any other divine being (see pp. 24–35)—has been a common feature of many Hindu communities in the last two millennia.

At least three factors contributed to the spread of such devotion. One was the use of vernacular languages, rather than Sanskrit. A second factor was its appeal across all social classes. Thirdly, from at least the fourth or fifth centuries, there was a culture of building temples. Some of the most famous devotional poet-saints, such as Nammalvar in the eighth century CE in south India, and Tukaram in the fifteenth, composed in vernacular languages and are perceived as having been from low castes. Yet their influence cut across all levels of a highly stratified society, their simplicity of worship appealing to the elite and masses alike. Other popular *bhakti* poets came from a wealthier social milieu. One of the most famous, Mira (1450?–1547 CE), was a Gujarati princess who wrote passionate poetry about her love for the god Krishna. According to some legends, at the end of her life Mira merged with Krishna's icon in a temple.

Men and women built temples and endowed monies and lands to these institutions. Temples in India became the centers of devotion, rituals, poetry, music, dance, scholarship, and economic distribution, as well as prestige markers for patrons. Many of the temples were centers of art, and, according to many scholars, also for astronomy.

An important development in the first millennium CE was the spread of the Hindu traditions to southeast Asia. Large temple complexes following precise ritual regulations were built in Cambodia, Indonesia, and other places. Hinduism flourished in these places until about the fifteenth century CE.

Along with the devotional and temple-building movements, philosophical studies of traditional Hindu texts flourished after the seventh century CE. The *Upanishad*s, the *Bhagavad Gita*, and another text called the *Brahma Sutra* were singled out for attention and commentarial interpretation. These texts form the nexus around which philosophical traditions, generically known as Vedanta, developed. Shankara (ca. eighth century), a major philosopher, spoke about the supreme being (*brahman*) and the human soul (*atman*) as identical with each other. The phenomenal reality we live in has limited validity, like dream states. Ramanuja (eleventh century) disagreed with Shankara and argued instead that the universe—that is, all sentient and non-sentient entities—forms the body of the supreme being, whom he identifies as Vishnu. There has been a long line of Vedanta philosophers that continues to this day.

After the fifteenth century, much of northern India came under Muslim rule (a dynasty known as the

The temple of Angkor Wat in modern-day Cambodia was built in the 12th century CE by King Suryavarman II, who dedicated it to Vishnu. The building follows the groundplan of a cosmic diagram or mandala.

Mughal, from "Mongol" due to its central Asian origins). While this led on the one hand to a meeting of cultures in art, music, and architecture, several Hindu temples were also destroyed in this period. In the sixteenth century, the Portuguese, Dutch, English, and French began to establish trading settlements in India. In time, as Mughal power disintegrated, the Europeans acquired territory, and in the eighteenth century large parts of the subcontinent became loosely unified under British control. Many social and religious practices of the Hindus—in particular "idolatry" and the caste system—came in for severe criticism from European missionaries and others. One response to external criticism came in the shape of reform movements that arose within Hinduism in the early modern period.

Ram Mohan Roy (1772–1833) and Dayanand Sarasvati (1824–1883) established movements to initiate educational, social, and religious reform. Of particular significance in the nineteenth century is Ramakrishna, whose many mystical experiences and teachings inspired leaders like Vivekananda. Vivekananda attended the First Parliament of Religions held in Chicago in 1893 and preached his experience of philosophical Hinduism in North America.

The many traditions that make up the tapestry of Hinduism continue to flourish in the diaspora. Hindus who migrated to southeast Asia in the first millennium CE sought to transmit their culture through the building of the great temples of Cambodia and Java. Similarly, Hindu émigrés to Britain and the United States in the past few decades have sought to perpetuate their culture into the new millennium through the religious and cultural nuclei of their own community temples.

In Praise of the *Bhagavata Purana*

❝ Narada asked: 'Who are you? Who are these two [men accompanying you]? And who are these women with lotus eyes?' . . .

The Lady replied: 'I am known as Devotion (*bhakti*). These men are Knowledge and Renunciation and are like my sons. They are old and worn out. These [women] are the rivers like Ganga and others who serve me . . . Listen to my story . . . I was born in the Dravida and came of age in Karnataka. I was respected in Maharashtra, but coming into Gujarat, I have become old and feeble. In this terrible eon called *kali*, I am crippled by heretics and their practices . . . It is after I reached Vrindavana that I have become young again and filled with beauty. My sons are anguished and sleep in exhaustion . . . they have become old and feeble.' . . .

[Narada soothes Lady Devotion and assures her that this evil age has at least one advantage:]

. . . Narada says: 'It is only in this age of Kali that a person can attain the supreme goal by reciting the name and speaking about the glory of Vishnu. This one cannot get even with austerities, yoga or meditation.' **❞**

A *mahatmyam* ("glory") of praise introducing the *Bhagavata Purana*, translated by Vasudha Narayanan.

Commentary

This passage, possibly added to the *Bhagavata Purana* (ca. 500 CE) several centuries after its composition, speaks of the spread of devotion from the south of India to the north. Although the earliest Sanskrit texts before the Common Era were composed in the north, vernacular devotional poetry became popular in the south after the sixth century CE and eventually moved north.

At least two points are significant in this passage. The first is a sectarian claim: that devotion to Vishnu is salvific in nature and devotion to Krishna (an incarnation of Vishnu), who lived in Vrindavana (in the north), is at the apex of Hindu movements. The second is the claim that the path of devotion rejuvenates itself, whereas those of knowledge and renunciation have become infirm. Although knowledge, meditation, yoga, and other forms of self-effort are lauded in texts, eventually it is devotional forms of worship that become the distinguishing character-istic of Hindu traditions—transmitted for centuries to the masses through singing and dancing lyrics of devotion.

The passage also alludes to the *kali yuga*, the worst possible era in the Hindu calculations of time. Time is cyclical, and this age of 432,000 years will be followed by the golden age. The unfolding of historical events is frequently juxtaposed against gigantic eons of time.

CHAPTER TWO

ASPECTS OF THE DIVINE

Hindus believe in many manifestations of the divine. Although most say they are monotheistic, their temples and domestic altars have multiple deities. In some Hindu texts, the supreme being is said to be ineffable and beyond name, gender, and form. Others perceive of the supreme as the perfect man or as a primordial mother. Some worship the divine being as half man, half female, or as a family of deities.

The belief that the divine is not only beyond gender and name, but also beyond number, has resulted in its manifestation in many shapes and forms: as human or animal, as trees, or as combinations of these beings. While the supreme being is beyond thought, most Hindus believe that she or he manifests him- or herself periodically on earth in order to protect the good and destroy evil.

LEFT: A gilded sculpture of the popular elephant-headed deity, Ganesha, stands on the grounds of the Festival of India in Middlesex County, New Jersey. Ganesha, son of Shiva and Parvati, is Hinduism's Lord of Beginnings and Remover of Obstacles. He is revered for his wisdom and courage.

The towns and cities of India may have dozens of temples and shrines dedicated to many deities. But images of gods and goddesses are also prominently displayed in stores, hospitals, and government offices, and on altars and shrines in Hindu homes.

Hindus may acknowledge many deities, but consider only one to be supreme; or they may consider all gods and goddesses equal, but worship one who is their favorite. However, many Hindus consider all divinities to be manifestations of a single godhead. For some, to say that this God is male or female, one or many, is to limit it, to impose human ideas of gender and number on the divine.

The supreme being is worshipped in temples in the form of an "image," a word often used (together with "idol") to translate the Sanskrit *murti*, which, however, is more accurately rendered as "form," or "embodiment." Most Hindus think of a sacred image as an actual incarnation of the supreme being, a form taken by the godhead in order to receive worship.

During a consecration ritual called *prana pratishta* ("establishment of life"), an image ceases to be gross matter and becomes an actual presence or incarnation of divinity on earth. The divine spirit is believed to remain in the icon for as long as devotees wish. Some Hindus, however, perceive an icon as a symbol pointing to a reality external to it. Yet other communities have rejected the notion of worshipping a deity in the form of an icon.

The *Upanishad*s, Hindu sacred texts composed ca. 600 BCE (see p. 38), refer to the supreme being as *brahman*, which is considered to be ineffable and beyond all human comprehension. For centuries, the definition of *brahman* has been the subject of intense speculation. *Brahman*, according to the *Taittiriya Upanishad*, is truth (*satya*), knowledge (*jñana*), and infinity (*ananta*). Beyond this, all that can be expressed about *brahman* is that it is existence (*sat*), consciousness (*chit*), and bliss (*ananda*). Ultimately, *brahman* cannot be described, since to describe is to confine, and with the infinite, this is impossible. The sage Yajñavalkya said that, paradoxically, one may come close to describing *brahman* only by stating what it is not.

A similar difficulty surrounds any definition of the relationship between *brahman* and *atman* (the human soul). In a famous dialogue in the *Chandogya Upanishad*, a father asks his son to dissolve salt in water. The father says that *brahman* and *atman* are united in a similar manner and ends his teaching with a famous dictum: "*Tat tvam asi*" (Sanskrit, "You are that"). "That" (*tat*) refers to *brahman* and "you" (*tvam*) to *atman*. The philosopher Shankara (eighth century CE) believed this statement to imply that *brahman* and *atman* are identical. But Ramanuja (eleventh century CE) saw it as indicating that *brahman* and *atman* are inseparable, but not identical.

Although the *Upanishad*s consider *brahman* to be beyond human comprehension, the texts called the *Purana*s ("Ancient [Lore]") claim that this divine entity assumes a form and name to make itself accessible to humankind—hence Hindus speak of the supreme being as both *nirguna* ("without attributes") and *saguna* ("with attributes," such as grace and mercy). Texts identify the supreme being variously as Vishnu ("All-Pervasive"), Shiva ("Auspicious One"), or the Goddess in one of her many manifestations, such as Shakti ("Energy"), Durga, and Kali.

Hindus have continuously venerated the divine in female form—very often referred to simply as the Goddess—for more than two thousand years. The Goddess, sometimes called Devi in Sanskrit literature, is usually seen as a manifestation of Parvati, the wife of Shiva. As a beneficent deity, she is frequently called Amba or Ambika ("Little Mother"), and is widely venerated as Shri or Lakshmi (see p. 28). As Kali, the Goddess is dark and awe-inspiring, garlanded with a

The god Vishnu is shown resting on the coils of a seven-headed snake symbolizing eternity in this painting in the Lakshminarayan Temple, Orchha, Madhya Pradesh, northern India. Brahma, representing Vishnu's creative energy, hovers in the center (top) while Lakshmi, Vishnu's consort, is at his feet.

necklace of skulls. Even in this form, she is called "mother" by her devotees.

As a warrior goddess, she is Durga, depicted with a smiling countenance but wielding an array of weapons. Durga, riding a tiger or lion, is one of the most popular goddesses in India. Strong and beautiful, the weapons in her hand show her readiness to assist her devotees. In one celebrated story, she manifests herself with the energies of all other deities in order to combat a buffalo-demon, Mahisa Asura. She emerges victorious after nine nights of struggle, commemorated by the festival of Navaratri ("Nine Nights") in the fall (see pp. 78–79).

Perhaps the best known manifestation of the Goddess in the Hindu and Jain traditions is Shri, more popularly known as Lakshmi. She is the goddess of wealth and good fortune and her picture graces millions of homes, shops, and businesses. Shri-Lakshmi is called the mother of all creation, bestower of wisdom and salvation, and grace incarnate. She brings good fortune on this earth, but above all she is instrumental in granting liberation from the cycle of life and death. Lakshmi is said to bestow wealth and saving grace just by glancing at a person. While she is depicted as an independent goddess, and has her own shrine in many temples, she is often also portrayed as the inseparable consort of Vishnu.

Shri-Lakshmi is frequently associated with the lotus. She is all-pervasive, latent in everything, but manifests herself only in auspicious places, of which the lotus is a great example. The flower (and its leaves) reminds human beings of how to regard their relationship to the world: it rises from mud and dirty water, yet is never tainted by them.

In some regions, a goddess may be known only by a local name and celebrated in stories with a local setting; elsewhere, she may be identified with a pan-Hindu goddess. In addition to the many pan-Hindu goddesses there are hundreds of regional ones worshipped by local communities. Some communities may offer animal sacrifices to their local village goddesses or Kali.

The local manifestations of the pan-Hindu gods and goddesses have distinctive histories and functions. Thus Vishnu is known in many parts of south India by specifically regional names. Lord Venkateswara, a manifestation of Vishnu in Tirupati, is one of the most popular deities in south India, and temples to him are seen in many parts of India and the United States.

Although Vishnu, Shiva, and the Goddess are the most important deities in Hindu texts, there are many other deities throughout India. The elephant-headed Ganesha (a son of Parvati), Kartikkeya/Murugan (a son of Shiva), and Hanuman (a divine monkey-devotee of Rama, an incarnation of Vishnu), are some of the more popular deities in Hinduism. Many roadside shrines are dedicated to Ganesha and Hanuman. Ganesha is also called Vigneshwara ("He who overcomes all obstacles"). Hindus worship him before embarking on any task, project, or journey.

Gods and goddesses all have their own iconographic characteristics, and every position of the hands or feet, every associated animal, plant, or bird, has a special significance. One of Lakshmi's hands, for instance, points to the ground in what Hindus refer to as the *varada* ("giving") position. In Hindu art, she may be portrayed giving wealth to her devotees, with a shower of gold coins emanating from her hand. The other hand may be held upright, denoting her protection of the devotee. Many deities have several hands, each carrying a weapon or a flower to protect his or her devotees from harm. Some Hindus interpret the numerous arms of a deity as representing omnipotence.

Most deities are associated with one or more animals. Although sacred texts give specific mythological reasons for their presence, believers may understand them more metaphorically. Thus, Ganesha's elephant head and mouse companion are sometimes said to represent his power to overcome hindrances: an elephant crushes large obstacles, and a mouse gnaws through little ones. Like Ganesha, many deities have specific functions, so a person may worship one god or goddess in order to achieve success in their career, another to cure illness, and so on.

Devotees of a deity may perceive him or her to be the supreme being. Some early writings express the idea of a divine trinity (*trimurti*) of Brahma (the creator), Vishnu (the preserver), and Shiva (the destroyer), but this concept was never widely popular. In time, Brahma became marginal, and the functions of creation, preservation, and destruction were combined in one deity—either Vishnu, Shiva, or Devi (the Goddess), depending on the individual devotee.

The manifold aspects of Shiva's power are expressed in his often paradoxical roles; he is both fierce and benevolent, creator and destroyer, exuberant dancer and austere *yogi*, ascetic and husband of the goddess Parvati. Stories of his powers of salvation present him as granting wisdom and grace to his devotees. Iconographically, Shiva and Parvati are portrayed in the abstract form symbolizing the male and female generative powers.

Vishnu is portrayed as having a multiplicity of incarnations (Sanskrit *avatara*, "descent"). It is believed that over the ages he has descended to earth several times in various animal and human forms to overthrow evil and establish *dharma*, or righteousness. Hindus generally consider ten incarnations to be the most important. Vishnu's first descent was as a fish that saved Manu (the progenitor of the human race), his family, and many animals from a flood. Vishnu was subsequently incarnated as a tortoise, a boar, a creature that was half lion and half man, and a dwarf-being.

The four fully human incarnations of Vishnu follow: the warrior Parasurama; Rama (the hero of a great epic, the *Ramayana*; see pp. 39–41); Balarama; and Krishna. It is believed that the tenth incarnation will come at the end of the present world age, which according to some reckonings began ca. 3102 BCE and will last 432,000 years. Some texts omit Balarama and introduce the Buddha as the ninth incarnation, after Krishna. The progression of the incarnations from fish to full human is understood by some Hindus today as anticipating evolutionary theory. But the more prevalent explanation is that Vishnu takes the form most suited for the crisis on hand.

Vishnu's ninth incarnation, Krishna ("the Dark One"), is one of the most popular Hindu gods. He is widely celebrated in folksongs, narratives (such as the *Bhagavad Gita*), sculpture, painting, and performance. While Krishna is generally perceived to be an incarnation of Vishnu, several traditions think of him as the supreme deity.

One such group is the International Society for Krishna Consciousness (ISKCON), which was founded in 1966 by A.C. Bhaktivedanta (born Abhaycharan De, 1896–1977) in New York. The theology of this movement (which is more popularly known as "Hare Krishna"), and its devotional chanting, may be traced back directly to the great guru Chaitanya (1486–1583). Members of ISKCON study the *Bhagavad Gita* (see pp. 41–42) and the stories of Vishnu in the *Bhagavata Purana*.

To some extent, most Hindus accept Krishna's supremacy among the incarnations of Vishnu, considering him to be what is termed the "full" descent of the deity. Krishna is also the alluring lover, dancing moonlit nights away with adoring cowherd maidens. Their dances are reenacted in many communities: the Gujarati *raas lila* dances are particularly renowned.

Many Hindus attribute divine status to the earth as well as to natural phenomena. Rivers like the Ganga (Ganges), Kaveri, Yamuna, and others, are personified and worshipped as mother goddesses. Hindus also revere heavenly bodies and propitiate the *navagraha* ("nine planets"—the sun, the moon, Venus, Mercury, Mars, Jupiter, Saturn, and two mythical entities called Rahu and Ketu) in rituals. Many temples in south India and in the diaspora incorporate images of the planets.

How Many Gods Are There?

“ Vidagha Shakalyah asked: 'Yajnavalkya, how many gods
are there?' He answered . . . in line with the ritual prayer,
'. . . three hundred and three, and three and three thousand.'
'Yes, but Yajnavalkya, how many gods are there, really?'
'Thirty-three.'
'Yes, but really, how many gods are there, Yajnavalkya?'
'Six.'
'Yes, but really, how many gods are there, Yajnavalkya?'
'Three.' . . .
'Yes, but really, how many gods are there, Yajnavalkya?'
'One and a half.'
'Yes, but really, how many gods are there, Yajnavalkya?'
'One.'
'Yes, but who are those three hundred and three and
three thousand and three?'
'They are but the powers/greatness of the gods; but
there are only thirty-three gods.' ”

Brihadaranyaka Upanishad III.9.1–2 (ca. 6th century BCE, Sanskrit), translated by Vasudha Narayanan.

Commentary

From a refusal to attribute gender or number to limit
the infinity of the supreme being to glowing praise for
various deities, the Hindu tradition has prose and poetry

to meet an array of philosophical and devotional aspirations. In the passage quoted, the theologian Yajnavalkya is asked how many gods there are. Replying with a formulaic number, usually given as three hundred and thirty million gods, Yajnavalkya is pressed again and again by the interrogator. His final answer seems to be "one," but he adds that all the deities are the powers of the gods and says there are thirty-three deities—an answer that is somewhat ambiguous.

Hundreds of verses in Sanskrit and vernacular languages muse at the ineffability of the supreme. Yet most Hindus also believe that the supreme being takes name and form and manifests him- or herself to devotees. Thus, the supreme power spoken of in the *Upanishad*s as "Brahman" is identified with Vishnu, Shiva, or a goddess, and in addition to these, several other gods and goddesses are also worshipped. The goddess Lakshmi, for example, is associated with salvific grace, compassion, and wealth. One of the most beloved of deities, she is worshipped in her own shrine in temples and is also seen as inseparable from Lord Vishnu. Icons of Lakshmi and the other deities were seen at home altars and in temple architecture in India and southeast Asia in the first millennium CE, and are now present all over the world.

CHAPTER THREE

SACRED TEXTS

Sacred texts in Hinduism have primarily been transmitted through music, recitation, dance, and drama. The higher castes of society consider the *Veda*s to be revealed, and in later centuries, several Sanskrit and vernacular texts were hailed as equivalent to these texts. Epic stories and narratives of deities have been conveyed through devotional poetry composed by men and women—these are popular not just in India but all over southeast Asia.

Sanskrit has been the language of the earliest texts. But many castes pay more attention to local bardic poetry and narratives. While there are several Sanskrit texts of law and ethics (*dharma*), Hindus consider custom and practice to be at least as important as these texts. In addition to Sanskrit texts, vernacular literature is beloved by all Hindus.

LEFT: The principles of many Indian classical dance forms have their origins in the Hindu sacred texts, the Vedas. *For centuries, texts such as these have been transmitted to the masses via the medium of dance, which is considered a symbolic form of worship.*

The Hindu traditions have a multiplicity of sacred texts in Sanskrit and regional languages. These have been commented upon, committed to memory, sung, choreographed, danced, and expressed in art and architecture. The oldest Indian sacred texts are the *Veda*s, ordinarily dated around or sometimes earlier than 1500 BCE. Each of the four Vedic collections (*Rig Veda*, *Sama Veda*, *Yajur Veda*, and *Atharva Veda*) comprises hymns and ritual treatises, together with *Aranyaka*s ("Compositions for the Forest") and *Upanishad*s ("Sitting Near [the Teacher]"), philosophical works composed ca. 600 BCE or a little later.

Some Hindu traditions consider the *Veda*s to be trans-human, that is, not authored by human beings. They are said to be eternal in nature and revealed in every cycle of time. The Vedic reciters, or "seers" (*rishi*s), did not invent or compose the *Veda*s; they "saw," or "envisaged," them. The seers transmitted them to their disciples, starting an oral tradition that has come down to the present. The order of the sacred words must remain fixed, and committing them to memory is a disciplined process involving the use of many mnemonic devices to ensure accurate pronunciation, rhythm, and diction.

The Vedic corpus was followed by the *smriti* or "remembered" literature. Although of human authorship, *smriti* was nonetheless considered inspired, and while of lesser authority than the *Vedas*, it has played a far more important role in the lives of the Hindus over the last two and a half millennia. The *smriti* is sometimes divided into the categories of epics, ancient stories (*Puranas*), and codes of law and ethics (*dharmashastras*; "texts on righteous behavior;" see pp. 99–100).

The two *smriti* epics, the *Ramayana* ("Story of Rama") and the *Mahabharata* ("Great Epic of India" or, alternatively, "Great Sons of Bharata"), are the best known works of the Hindu tradition. These works, with ethical, spiritual, narrative, philosophic, and cosmogonic content, have been interpreted, commented upon, and enjoyed for over two thousand years and form the heart of Hindu sacred literature. For many Hindus, the phrase "sacred books" connotes these epics in particular, and for countless Hindu children the narration of the epics is invariably their first and most lasting encounter with Hindu scripture.

The *Ramayana* focuses on the prince Rama (later portrayed as an incarnation of Vishnu), who is born in Ayodhya. On the eve of his coronation, his father Dasaratha exiles him. In the forest, Rama's wife, Sita, is captured by Ravana, the demon king of Lanka, and the epic focuses on Rama's struggle to win her back. After

An illustration, ca. 1830, depicting a scene from the
Ramayana. *The epic's eponymous hero, Rama, is shown*
standing before kings and holy men (rishis) *holding a bow.*

a battle, Rama kills Ravana and is reunited with Sita.
They eventually return to Ayodhya and are crowned.
Rama is held to be an ideal king.

There have been many vernacular versions of the
Ramayana, and the story has been understood in various
ways. In one thirteenth-century interpretation, Sita
voluntarily undergoes captivity and suffering to rescue
other human beings and the world from evil. In a

metaphorical reading, the human soul (Sita) is captured by the material body (Ravana), which is defeated by Rama, who saves the soul from the clutches of the senses. Some versions of the tale, called the *Sitayana*, tell the story from Sita's viewpoint. The *Ramayana* is danced out and acted in places of Hindu (and Buddhist) cultural influence in southeast Asia, and its characters are well known in Cambodia, Thailand, and Indonesia.

With around one hundred thousand verses, the *Mahabharata* is considered the world's longest poem. It is the story of the great struggle among the descendants of a king called Bharata (whose name is used by many Indians to mean "India"). The main part of the poem deals with a war between two families, the Pandavas and the Kauravas. The Kauravas try to cheat the Pandavas out of their share of the kingdom, and a great battle ensues that forces every kingdom to take sides. The Pandavas emerge victorious, but at great cost—all their sons and close relatives die in the battle.

Few Hindu households will have the *Mahabharata*, but many will have a copy of a celebrated episode contained within it—the *Bhagavad Gita* ("Sacred Song"), one of the holiest books in the Hindu tradition. Just as the war of the *Mahabharata* is about to begin, Arjuna, one of the Pandava brothers (hitherto portrayed as a hero who has emerged victorious from battle), becomes distressed at the thought of having to fight his relatives.

Arjuna asks his cousin Krishna (who is portrayed as an incarnation of Vishnu) whether it is correct to fight a war in which many lives, especially of one's own kin, are to be lost. Krishna replies in the affirmative: it is correct if one fights for righteousness (*dharma*). The Pandavas had earlier tried peaceful ways of negotiation. The conversation on the field of battle between Krishna and Arjuna takes up about eighteen chapters and constitutes the *Bhagavad Gita*.

The *Gita* says one may reach Vishnu/Krishna/God through devotion, knowledge, or selfless action. Later interpreters think of these as three paths, while others consider them to be three aspects of the one path of loving surrender to the supreme being. Krishna also instructs Arjuna—who is generally understood to represent any human soul who seeks guidance—on the nature of the soul, God, and how one can reach liberation.

The epics and the *Purana*s are written in Sanskrit, the ancient "perfected" language, which, rather like Latin for many centuries in Europe, was largely the province of male members of the social elites. However, in India, men and women of other castes voiced their devotional passion and quest for divine compassion in local tongues. Today, India has over eighteen official languages and hundreds of dialects, and many of them have a long and rich history of religious literature.

The earliest Hindu religious texts in a vernacular language are in Tamil, a south Indian language spoken by more than seventy-five million people today. A sophisticated body of literature in Tamil existed two thousand years ago. The oldest works, usually referred to as *Sangam* ("Academy") poems, are secular texts about kings and chivalry or love and romance. These became the model for later devotional literature, where the deity was cast in the role of a ruler and lover.

Hindu *bhakti* (devotional) literature flourished in south India after the sixth century CE. Saints traveled from temple to temple singing hymns in Tamil in praise of Vishnu or Shiva. These hymns, which are Hinduism's earliest sacred works in the vernacular, draw on earlier Tamil poetry and address the deity in highly personal, intimate, and tender language. In the vernacular literature, Vishnu and his incarnations (see pp. 31–32) and Shiva are cast in several different roles by the devotee, who considers the deity to be a father or mother, lover, bridegroom, protector, or innermost soul. Sometimes the deity is even portrayed as a young child, to whom the devotee sings with maternal love.

After the tenth century, Tamil devotional poems were introduced into temple liturgy in Tamil-speaking areas and were regarded as being equivalent in status to the Sanskrit *Veda*s. Devotionalism spread to the west and north of India after the eleventh century CE, transmitted through sacred texts such as the *Bhagavata Purana*, as well as through the figure of Ramananda (1299?–1400), a legendary devotee in Ramanuja's line. In the thirteenth century, the poet Jñaneshvar discussed the ideals of the *Bhagavad Gita* in a famous treatise that bears his name, the *Jñaneshvari*, composed in Marathi, the language of the Maharashtra region.

Several features contributed to the spread of vernacular devotion. One was the use of contemporary living languages. A second was its appeal across all social classes. A third was the building of hundreds of temples, which also increased pilgrimage traditions and supported devotional rituals. Surdas (ca. 1483–1563), a blind singer and poet, composed in a dialect of Hindi. In his *Sursagar*, the youthful Krishna is celebrated in lyrics popular among many Hindus. Another important vernacular devotional writer was Tulsidas (1543?–1623), who settled in Varanasi. His *Lake of the Deeds of Rama* was more than a recounting or translation of the *Ramayana*. Its widely known verses have their own beauty and have inspiried hundreds of traditional storytellers and millions of Rama devotees in Hindi-speaking areas.

The spread of the devotional compositions all over India challenged the orthodox claim that Sanskrit was the exclusive vehicle for revelation and theological communication. While some *brahmin*s have always learned and hence kept alive large sections of the Sanskrit Vedic tradition, others may know only a few Sanskrit hymns. However, overwhelming numbers of Hindus can recite devotional verses in their own languages. The Hindi poems of Surdas on Krishna, the songs of Princess Mira, and the Tamil poems of Nammalvar and Andal (eighth–ninth centuries CE), may serve as scripture for a particular community. In this sense, vernacular poems and songs guide, inspire, console, and offer hope and wisdom to the mass of the faithful more directly than the *Veda*s and other Sanskrit writings.

This is not to say that the vernacular literature is considered to be at variance with the message of the *Veda*s. Rather, in most communities, there is a belief that the holy people who composed in the living tongues gathered the truth from the incomprehensible *Veda*s and made it accessible to everyone, inspiring devotion and hastening the attainment of divine, saving grace.

The Songs of Andal

" A thousand elephants circle,

as Narana, Lord of virtues,

walks through the town in front of me.

Golden jars brim with water;

Festive flags and pennants,

    fly through this town

eager to welcome him—

I saw this in my dream, my friend!

Drums beat happy sounds; conches were blown.

Under the canopy strung heavy with pearls,

Madhusuda, my love, filled with virtue,

came and clasped the palm of my hand.

I saw this in my dream, my friend!

Those with eloquent mouths recited the good *Veda*s.

With *mantra*s they placed

the green leaves and the grass in a circle.

The lord, strong as a raging elephant,

softly held my hand as we circled the fire.

I saw this in my dream, my friend! "

Nacchiyar Tirumoli 1.1 and 1.6–7, by Andal (a woman poet, ca. ninth century CE, Tamil);
translated by Vasudha Narayanan.

Commentary

Over the last four thousand years, Hindu sacred texts have been transmitted in India and southeast Asia through ritual, music, and dance, rather than through sermons—the performing arts are seen as a means to liberation. The songs of Andal are important for south Indian Vishnu devotees, in the United States as well as in India. Like many poets, she is regionally well known, and some devotees consider her poems to be as significant as the *Upanishad*s, which are part of the *Veda*s.

While the most exalted texts are the *Veda*s, a great number of Hindus know their tradition through local versions of the epic narratives, and many experience devotion through the words of a local saint. In the *Nacchiyar Tirumoli* ("Sacred Words of the Lady"), Andal refuses to marry a human being and instead recounts a dream in which she marries Vishnu, whom she addresses by several other names. By the tenth century, theologians considered Andal to be a paradigmatic devotee. Every human being is considered to be like Andal and Vishnu is the bridegroom. Her icon is consecrated in Vaishnava temples and her songs are regularly recited in weddings in some communities in south India. They are also, like those of many vernacular poets in India, sung, choreographed, and danced at homes and in temples.

CHAPTER FOUR

SACRED PERSONS

In the Hindu tradition, deities descend to the earth as human beings and human beings ascend to a divine status. Salvific truth is said to be mediated by these holy persons. The earliest holy men and women who "saw" the truth and compiled the *Veda*s were called "seers." Although the many lineages of holy teachers in Hinduism were composed of men of the brahmin caste, hundreds of saints and charismatic people considered to be *"guru*s" have come from all castes of society. In many Hindu communities, the sacred teacher is considered to be as important as the deity and is venerated, and even worshipped; other communities, however, do not consider the teacher to be so significant. From the twentieth century, women *guru*s took on an increasingly significant role, and many are now viewed as deities.

LEFT: Maharishi Mahesh Yogi (born 1911), the founder of the Transcendental Movement, is arguably one of Hinduism's most influential figures. He is widely accredited with having introduced Hindu philosophy to the West.

Hindus have long looked to holy men and women to instruct them on how to attain peace in this lifetime and, eventually, liberation from the endless cycle of life and death (see pp. 90–91). For many Hindus, the primary religious experience is mediated by a teacher who may be called *acharya*, *guru*, or *swami*. The term *acharya* usually denotes the formal head of a monastery, sect, or subsect, or a teacher who initiates a disciple into a movement. Sometimes the word is used simply as a synonym for *guru*, which, like *swami* ("master"), is a looser and more widespread term for any religious teacher. There are also thousands of ascetics, individuals possessed by a deity or spirit, mediums, storytellers, and *sadhu*s ("holy men"), who all command the veneration of their followers.

Each of the many Hindu philosophical traditions forms a distinct sect and has its own leader. Often the leadership of Hindu groups has passed from teacher to teacher in a line of succession that has continued for centuries down to the present day. This is the case with, for example, the schools founded by Shankara (ca. eighth century), Ramanuja (eleventh century), Madhva (thirteenth century), and Chaitanya (sixteenth century). Schisms often occur in such communities, with complementary or competing leaders vying for the loyalty of the disciples. Both ascetic monastic leaders as well as married men from specific lineages have followers in many Vaishnava (devotees of Vishnu) communities.

Shankara is said to have established four or five monasteries in different parts of India: at Dvaraka (west), Puri (east), Sringeri and Kanchipuram (south), and Badrinath (north). In each of these monasteries there is a lineage of teachers, all of whom bear the title "Shankara the Teacher" (Shankaracharya). They have often engaged with social and political issues, and exercise considerable leadership among the educated urban population, as well as influencing those who adhere to the philosophy of their founder. A similar role is played by intellectual philosophical commentators such as Swami Chinmayananda, whose followers have been active in the preservation of traditional scriptures in print and electronic media. In the Ramanuja school, as part of a complex initiation ritual, the leader brands a new member lightly on the shoulders and gives him or her a new name and a personal *mantra* for meditation. However, membership in other devotional communities may be much more informal.

At any given time, there are many influential theologians, and new sects with substantial followings arise under the inspiration of charismatic *guru*s in almost every generation. Although the distinction may not be clear in the minds of followers, it is possible to distinguish between those spiritual leaders who belong to ancient or more recent lineages, and charismatic teachers who attract devotees through "supernatural" phenomena ranging from the "magical" manifestation of objects to faith healing. Such leaders defy straightforward classification, and each has a large following. Devotees sometimes consider these *gurus* to be an incarnation of a divinity, who has descended to earth in the form of their teacher for the welfare of humanity. This is the case with Sri Satya Sai Baba (born Satya Narayan Raju, 1926), a charismatic leader from Andhra Pradesh, who is believed by his followers to be an incarnation of the deities Shiva and Shakti (the Goddess).

Several female *gurus* have acquired large followings of devotees. Among the most famous are Anandamayi Ma (1896–1982), a Bengali, and Amritanandamayi Ma (born 1953). Such teachers often lead celibate lives. Many charismatic teachers who do not come from a lineage of institutionalized *gurus* are said to have been born divine. Some devotees revere their teachers simply as spiritually elevated and highly evolved souls, beings who have ascended above the cares of human life to a state of self-realization or perfection. Occasionally, a

Female devotees gather in Bhajan Ashram. Since the twentieth century, women have taken an increasingly prominent role in Hindu religion.

charismatic religious leader may have a title such as *rishi* ("seer"), like the composers of the *Veda*s. One well-known example is Mahesh Yogi (born 1911), the founder of the Transcendental Meditation movement—popularly referred to in the West as "TM"—who is known as the Maharishi, or "Great Seer."

Today, many *guru*s have Internet sites maintained by devotees; their itineraries, sermons, and songs are broadcast through these web pages, creating a world-wide Hindu "cyber-community."

"*Acharya devo bhava*": Consider Your Teacher as God

❝ I bow to the lineage of teachers (*guru*s)

which begins with the Lord of Lakshmi

with Nathamuni and Yamuna in the middle;

I take refuge with my teacher! **❞**

❝ Even if they are lower than the four castes

that uphold all clans

even outcastes to outcastes

without a trace of virtue

if they are the servants of the servants

who have mingled in service with the Lord

with the wheel in his right hand

his body dark as blue sapphire

they are our masters. **❞**

Laudatory invocation attributed to Kuresa (11th century CE, Sanskrit) and Nammalvar's *Tiruvaymoli* 3.7.9, translated by Vasudha Narayanan.

Commentary

Perhaps more than any other religious tradition, Hinduism recognizes divinity in human beings. Many spiritual teachers are considered to be souls who have ascended to be one with the supreme being; others think of holy men and women as the descent of the divine being to earth. For some disciples, the teachers are even more important than God. The Upanishadic dictum (*Tait-tiriya Upanishad*) to treat your teacher as God is well known by millions of Hindus.

Almost every philosophical tradition has its own set of verses celebrating holy men and women. The first, invocatory verse quoted opposite, saluting a lineage of teachers, is recited by Sri Vaishnava Hindus at the beginning of all ritual prayer; it recognizes Lakshmi as one of the first teachers then begins with the poet Nammalvar (ca. ninth century) who is lauded in other verses. Nathamuni and Yamuna (ca. ninth and tenth centuries) are seen to be in the "middle" of the spiritual chain.

One does not have to be part of a spiritual lineage to be a holy person. In the second passage, Nammalvar identifies anyone who serves Vishnu as his master, even if they are of "low" caste. Since the last century, charismatic women *guru*s have become very prominent and command large followings. Some men and women perform miracles; others interpret scripture; some keep vows of silence; others encourage service to human beings. Holy men and women come with many teachings, are of all castes, and some of the more important ones are celebrated over hundreds of years. Some are enshrined in temples; others are remembered through their holy words and works.

CHAPTER FIVE

ETHICAL PRINCIPLES

Dharma, a concept central to Hinduism, has many meanings, including "duty," "righteousness," and "ethics." There is a *dharma* common to all humanity that is evident in such virtues as non-violence, compassion, and generosity. There is also a *dharma* that is specific to one's caste and station in life, and another that leads to liberation from the cycle of life and death.

In Hinduism, *karma* has come to mean the process whereby the good and bad deeds performed by human beings in the present determine the quality of their lives both now and in future births. Some Hindus believe that through detached action, and knowledge, one may gain liberation. Others maintain that through devotion and surrender one can acquire the saving grace of the supreme being, which stops the cycle of rebirth.

LEFT: *Hindu pilgrims bathing in the sacred waters of lake Pushkar, Rajasthan. The waters are believed to bring liberation from the cycle of rebirth. The town of Pushkar contains numerous Hindu temples, the most important of which is dedicated to the creator god, Brahma.*

In Hinduism, the Sanskrit word *dharma* has been used in many contexts, which include: one's duty according to one's caste, social class, or stage of life; a code of conduct that embraces, but is not limited to, regulations involving marriage, food, religious observance, and so on; virtues such as gratitude and compassion, which are thought of as common to all human beings; and a path to liberation from the cycle of life and death. The texts on *dharma* also form the basis for formulating the administration of Hindu family law in India.

Hindu texts list four sources as the foundations of *dharma*: the *Veda*s (see pp. 38–39); the epics—the texts of lore called the *Purana*s (see pp. 38–39); the behavior and practices of the good people; and finally, the promptings of one's mind or conscience. It is most significant that in the Hindu traditions, textual norms are not the only guide to ethics—local practices and customs are extremely important in understanding what is ethical and, in Hindu family law, what is legal.

Virtues that are said to be common to all human beings are called *sadharana* (common) or *sanatana* (eternal) *dharma*. These include gratitude, non-violence, compassion, and generosity. Other forms of correct behavior depend on one's community and, sometimes, on one's stage of life, or ritual calendar. Thus most (although not all) Brahmins and Vaishnavas (followers of Vishnu) are vegetarians all the time; others eat fish, fowl, and certain kinds of meat, except during certain times in the lunar calendar.

Within Hinduism itself, among several possible routes to liberation, two broad perspectives stand out. The first characterizes Hindu traditions that believe the human soul to be identical with the supreme being. Liberation is the final experiential knowledge that we are divine. This world view, best described by the teacher Shankara (see pp. 50–51), emphasizes the importance of human effort and striving in achieving the necessary transforming wisdom. The second perspective comes from the schools that speak of an ultimate distinction, however tenuous, between the human being and God. Proponents of this view advocate devotion to the supreme being and reliance on God's grace.

In the course of the *Bhagavad Gita* (see pp. 41–42), Krishna describes three ways to liberation: the way of action; the way of knowledge; and the way of devotion. Some Hindus view these as multiple paths to the divine, others as aspects of one discipline. The way of action (*karma yoga*) is the path of unselfish action; a person must do his or her duty (*dharma*), such as studying or good deeds, but not out of fear of blame or punishment,

मह्रेद्र्यासन १२

An 18th-century Indian miniature painting depicting a yogi sitting astride an animal skin in meditation posture. In Hinduism, yoga is a mode of spiritual progress and a means of attaining liberation.

or hope of praise or reward. In thus discarding the fruits of one's action, one attains abiding peace. This entails acting altruistically for the good of humanity and performing all actions in a compassionate manner.

According to the way of knowledge (*jñana yoga*), by attaining scriptural knowledge one may achieve a transforming wisdom that destroys one's past *karma* (see pp. 90–93). This wisdom may be acquired through the learning of texts from a suitable teacher (*guru*), meditation, and physical and mental control in the form of the discipline of *yoga*.

The third way to liberation is that most emphasized in the *Bhagavad Gita*: the way of devotion (*bhakti yoga*). It is widely popular among Hindus of every walk of life.

The Sanskrit term *yoga* refers to the practice of various disciplines whereby a devotee "yokes" his or her spirit to the divine. It is held in high regard in Hindu texts, and has had many meanings. Patañjali's *yoga* (ca. third century BCE), as interpreted by commentators, involves moral, mental, and physical discipline, and meditation. This form of *yoga* is described as having eight "limbs," or disciplines, including restraint from violence, falsehood, and other negative practices, as well as positive practices such as equanimity and asceticism.

Patañjali also recommends bodily postures for meditation, and the practice of breath control (*pranayama*) and mental detachment from external stimuli. Concentration and meditation (*dhyana*) lead to *samadhi*, the final state of union with the divine and liberation from the cycle of life and death; it is a state that cannot be adequately described within the constraints of human language.

In the past century, a distinction has been drawn between *raja yoga* and *hatha yoga*. *Raja yoga* deals with mental discipline; occasionally, this term is used interchangeably with Patañjali's *yoga*. *Hatha yoga*, popular in the West, focuses on bodily postures and control. Final liberation can be attained only after one harmonizes different centers in the body with the cosmos.

Instructions for Students of the *Veda*

❝ Speak the truth. Follow the path of righteousness. Do
not neglect your recitation of your *Veda* [or learning].
Having brought the wealth dear to your teacher, do not
cut your ties. Do not neglect truth. Do not neglect
Dharma. Do not neglect the well-being [of your body].
Do not neglect fortune and wealth. Do not neglect
study and teaching of sacred texts. Do not neglect the
rituals to honor gods and ancestors.

Consider your mother as god; consider your father
as god; consider your teacher as god; think of your
guests as gods.

Do those deeds that are without blame, not others.
Hold in esteem only the good that you have seen in us,
not other practices . . .

Give with faith; do not give without faith. Give in
plenty, give with modesty, give with fear, give with
full knowledge and compassion. **❞**

Taittiriya Upanishad 1.11.1–3, translated by Vasudha Narayanan.

Commentary

These words, recited by a teacher to a departing student,
are well known in many sectors of the Hindu tradition,
and even in this century, have been part of the graduation

exercises in some universities in India. The student is asked to practice daily recitation of the *Veda*—which in recent years has been interpreted loosely as "learning" something every day. It is not just textual knowledge that is advocated; one is asked to honor one's parents, teachers, and guests. The student is specifically told to act in a manner beyond reproach and to adopt those practices that seem to be in accord with *dharma* (righteousness) and those enacted with compassion.

Wealth is not scorned or held in contempt; one is asked to take care of one's health and wealth. Hinduism is life-affirming; celibacy and rejection of wealth are recommended only for young students, or for those in the later stages of life. Those who have finished their studies, on the other hand, are encouraged to marry, earn money, and take care of the welfare of all.

Generosity has always been a virtue that is celebrated in Hindu stories; the admonition here is to give with faith, to give with trepidation and compassion, for one can be, and frequently is, indirectly on the receiving end; one is not to give with arrogance or with ego. Several narratives highlight the importance of generous giving. The history of Hindu temple-building and maintenance is filled with the names of men and women who endowed monies with generosity.

CHAPTER SIX

SACRED SPACE

Mountains, groves, rivers, towns, cities, and forests are all considered sacred in the Hindu tradition. And although the entire south Asian sub-continent is thought to be holy, thousands of places claim a special status and have been visited by pilgrims for centuries. Many Hindus believe that they can gain liberation just by visiting a sacred place or by bathing in a holy river.

Temples were built according to strict regulations, facing specific auspicious directions. These temples and shrines display the embodied cosmologies of Hinduism, and some were built with precise astronomical coordination. The temples were centers of piety and power; they were also economic hubs and a nexus for cultural activities. The replication of holy places and sacralizing new territories have been hallmarks of Hindu migration.

LEFT: The magnificent 8th-century Shore temple in the coastal town of Mamalla-puram is dedicated to Shiva and has been a pilgrimage destination for centuries.

Millions of Hindus regularly visit sacred towns, worship in temples, bathe in holy rivers, and climb sacred mountains, in order to pray for happiness in this life and in the next. According to some Hindu texts, all of India is holy, as it is considered to be the place where the actions that form the basis of *karma* come to fulfillment. The idea of India as a sacred land began around the beginning of the Common Era. Manu, the author of a book on *dharma* (see pp. 58–59) and right behavior, defined a region south of the Himalayas and between the eastern and western oceans as the holy Aryavarta ("Country of the Noble Ones"). In time, the concept of the sacred land was extended to cover the whole subcontinent. Since the time of the early Sanskrit texts, India has been seen as a divine mother; in recent centuries, she has been hailed in many songs as "Mother India" (Bharata Mata) and as a compassionate mother goddess. This image has had political overtones: during the struggle for freedom from British rule, Mother India was portrayed as being held captive by foreign forces.

The map of India is filled with holy places. Although there are many standard Hindu pilgrimage itineraries, thousands of other towns, villages, and sites across India are also held sacred. Pilgrimage routes are often organized thematically: devotees might visit the one hundred and eight places where Shakti, or the power of the Goddess, is said to be present; the sixty-eight places where emblems of Shiva are said to have emerged "self-born"; the twelve places where he appears as the "flame of creative energies" (*jyotir linga*s); the eight places where Vishnu spontaneously manifested himself (*svayam vyakta*); and so on.

Hindu holy texts (see pp. 37–47), especially the epics and the *Purana*s, extol the sanctity of many individual sites. For pious Hindus, to live in such places, or to undertake a pilgrimage to one of them, is enough to destroy one's sins and assist in the attainment of liberation from the cycle of life, death, and rebirth (see pp. 89–93). A short verse known by millions of Hindus draws attention to seven of the most famous holy towns: "Ayodhya, Mathura, Maya, / Kashi, Kanchi, Avantika / And the city of Dvaraka; / These seven [cities] give us / Liberation."

Almost every holy place is associated with a *sthala purana*, a text that details the site's antiquity and sacredness. The temple itself is like a "port of transit," a place from where a human being may "cross over" (*tirtha*) the ocean of life and death. In fact, many temples and holy places are also located near the sea, a lake, a river, or a spring. When such a body of water is not close by, there is usually an artificial ritual well or pool, a feature that may date back to the time of the Harappan civilization (see p. 12)—the "Great Bath" of Mohenjo Daro resembles the pools that are attached to hundreds of Hindu temples in south India today. Pilgrims cleanse themselves physically and spiritually in these pools before praying in the temple.

The Ganga (Ganges), Yamuna, Kaveri, and Narmada rivers are believed to be so holy that merely by bathing in them one's sins are said to be destroyed. Confluences of two rivers or of a river and the sea are particularly sacred. Pilgrims journey regularly to bathe at Triveni Sangama ("Confluence of Three Rivers") at Prayag (Allahabad), where the Ganga, the Yamuna, and a mythical underground river, the Sarasvati, all meet. Small sealed jars of holy water from the Ganga are kept in homes and used in domestic rituals to purify the dead and dying.

The water from the Ganga, or another holy river in the north, may be taken to a sacred site in the far south, such as the coastal town of Rameswaram, and sand from Rameswaram may be taken back to the Ganga and immersed there. This practice serves to mark the completion of a circular pilgrimage and demonstrates one way in which the various holy places and traditions of Hinduism can be interlinked.

Varanasi on the river Ganga. This sacred city, the holiest in India, is visited by thousands every year. Immersion in the holy river is considered an act of great spiritual purification.

When temples are consecrated in Hindu communities outside India, water from Indian sacred rivers is mingled with water from rivers in the host country and poured onto the new temple, physically and symbolically connecting it with the sacred motherland.

Many holy sites are situated near mountains and caves, places where Hindu deities are said to reside in *Purana* stories. For example, Shiva lives on Mount Kailasa in the Himalayas, which for the devotee is represented by every Shiva temple. In some regions, particularly in the north, large temple towers (*shikharas*) represent these cosmic mountains. The innermost shrine of a Hindu temple is traditionally a windowless space, like the sacred caves that were among the earliest Hindu places of worship.

Although there is evidence of worship at temples dating from the beginning of the Common Era, large sacred complexes were built only after the sixth century CE. Migrants to southeast Asia also built temples to preserve and transmit their religion. Temples were major religious, cultural, and economic centers and were constructed according to elaborate rules to represent the whole cosmos. Some of the larger ones have seven enclosures, representing the seven layers of heaven present in Hindu cosmology.

Many temples, such as Angkor Wat in Cambodia, which was dedicated to Vishnu, also encoded measurements closely connected with Hindu systems of time measurement. A number of temples, of which Angkor Wat is one, were built in alignment with the position of certain stars and planets at particular times of the year and to observe and precisely measure astronomical phenomena.

Several of the temple complexes in India are associated with the major sects—that is, they enshrine

Vishnu, Shiva, or the Goddess and their entourages. In many of them, the deities are known by their local or regional names. A typical temple may have separate shrines for the deity, his or her spouse, other divine attendants, and saints. For example, an eighth-century CE temple in Tiruvanmiyur, a suburb of Chennai (Madras), has shrines for the main god, Shiva, his wife Parvati—known locally as Tripura Sundari ("Beautiful Lady of the Three Worlds")—and their children, Ganesha and Murugan. The temple also incorporates images of other manifestations of Shiva, such as Nataraja (the cosmic dancer) and icons of his devotees. Temples in the diaspora generally cater to a broader community of worshippers and have images of Shiva, Vishnu, the Goddess, and other deities enshrined under one roof.

India's richest temple—and one of the wealthiest religious institutions in the world—is the temple of Tirumala-Tirupati in Andhra Pradesh. Referred to in ancient literature as Tiru Venkatam, it is dedicated to Vishnu, who is popularly known as Venkateshvara ("Lord of the Venkatam hills"). Devotional literature addressed to Venkateshvara dates back to the seventh century CE, but pilgrims are known to have been visiting the site of the temple for almost two millennia. The temple is located in the scenic Tirumala hills and until

1965, when the government took them over, it owned more than six hundred surrounding villages.

Tirumala-Tirupati, like many large temples in India and southeast Asia, enjoyed the patronage of Indian royalty for over a thousand years. It is now a destination of large numbers of pilgrims. Annual donations of cash by pilgrims can amount to tens of millions of dollars. The temple employs its huge financial resources to fund a range of projects and enterprises, including charities, hospitals, universities and other educational institutions, housing developments, and publications. One major objective of the temple in recent years has been to contribute to the solution of India's considerable ecological problems, to which end it has subsidized massive reforestation projects.

Most Hindus attend their local temple or other holy place that has been important to their families for generations, or they may save for an extended pilgrimage to a famous distant sacred site. Émigrés and other devotees who cannot physically go on such a pilgrimage may watch the rituals that take place there on specially commissioned television programs or videos. At all times, Hindus can also worship at home, where a special area will very often be designated as the family's domestic worship space.

The human body itself is sometimes spoken of as the "temple of the supreme being." Some Hindu traditions, such as the Virashaivas (a community organized ca. 1150 CE), denounce temple worship and revere every human as the temple of the supreme being, Lord Shiva. Other traditions, for example south Indian communities that worship Vishnu and Lakshmi, uphold the practices of temple worship, but also think of the human body as divine. In one song, the eighth-century CE poet Periyalvar declared: "Build a temple in your heart. Install the lord called Krishna in it; Offer him the flower of love."

A holy space in the Hindu tradition is one in which devotees come to see the enshrined deity and hear sacred words from holy texts. In the past, religious teachers were careful about whom they imparted their teachings to, and screened their devotees carefully. But now, the Internet allows anyone to see images of deities, teachers, and gurus, and even hear the recitation and music of sacred texts and songs. Some websites call their home pages "electronic *ashram*s." An *ashram* was a traditional place of hermitage or learning. Internet images of deities are taken seriously by devotees; some websites remind Internet surfers that it would be disrespectful to download such images. The Internet may therefore be seen as the latest frontier of sacred space for many Hindus.

Heaven on Earth

❝ This is the temple of him who became
      the divine fish, tortoise, boar, lion, and dwarf.
      He became Rama in three forms, he became Kanna,
      and as Kalki he will end [these worlds].
This is Srirangam, where the swan and its mate
      swing on the lotus blossoms, embrace on flowery beds,
      and revel in the red pollen strewn around the river. **❞**

Periyalvar Tirumoli, 4.9.9 (ca. 9th century CE, Tamil), translated by Vasudha Narayanan.

❝ In the beautiful city of Ayodhya, encircled by towers,
A flame that lit up all the worlds appeared in the Solar
race, and gave life to all the heavens.
This warrior, with dazzling eyes,
Rama, dark as a cloud, the First one, my only lord,
is in . . . the City of Tillai.
    When is the day
    when my eyes behold him
    and rejoice? **❞**

Perumal Tirumoli, 10.1, by Kulasekhara Alvar, translated by Vasudha Narayanan.

Commentary

Many Hindu communities consider the temple and the sacred place to be an extension of heaven on earth, a place where hierophany took place. The consecrated icon of the deity is seen to be the actual body of the god or the goddess. Those in the south think of Srirangam (glorified in the first extract) as one of the most sacred places in the world. Tamil poets often sing about the natural beauty and wealth of the towns in which the deity is enshrined in a temple. Here, Periyalvar, a ninth-century Tamil saint, speaks of the swans, the lush flowers, and the red pollen, all of which exemplify a fertile land. It is in a temple in this land that Vishnu is enshrined. The Srirangam temple is like a hologram, containing the deity's ten manifestations and total divinity—a place that represents the descent of the deity to earth in order to facilitate the ascent of human beings to heaven.

In the second passage, Kulasekhara, a ninth/tenth-century poet writing in Tamil, glorifies the northern city of Ayodhya, the birthplace of Rama. However, the poet conceptualizes Rama as actually being enshrined in the city of Tillai (Chidambaram) in south India. These transpositions are common in devotional poetry—consequently, thousands of places in India, as well as in other parts of the world, are seen as sacred.

CHAPTER SEVEN

SACRED TIME

The Hindu calendar is filled with auspicious and propitious times on which to embark on journeys, start new enterprises, enter homes, get married, or have celebrations. Astrology is an integral part of Hindu life, and a child's horoscope is frequently cast as soon as she or he is born. There are times that are auspicious for everyone and others that are specific to individuals. Inauspicious times are also marked.

Festival days involve times of feasting and fasting. Important festivals include the birthdays of the gods Rama, Krishna, and Ganesha; Navaratri ("Nine Nights"), which marks the destruction of a demon by the goddess Durga; Dipavali ("Necklace of Lights"); and Pongal, a harvest festival in southern India. Hindus ordinarily follow a lunar calendar that is adjusted to the solar calendar.

LEFT: Sacred time in Hinduism is marked by an abundance of local festivals and rituals, many of which celebrate specific deities. At the festival shown here, a young Hindu man is dressed as Shiva, one of the tradition's most important gods (see p. 31).

Hindu festivals are filled with color and joy and almost always associated with feasting and pleasure, although they usually also involve periods of ritual fasting. The birthdays of the gods Rama, Krishna, and Ganesha are widely popular throughout India, while important regional festivals include Holi (a jubilant spring festival held in parts of northern India to celebrate the new colors of the springtime flowers), Onam (a harvest festival celebrated in the southern state of Kerala between August and September in honor of the fifth incarnation of the god Vishnu (see pp. 31–32), and Pongal (a mid-January harvest festival in Tamil Nadu).

The festival of Navaratri ("Nine Nights") is celebrated throughout India and begins on the new moon in the lunar month from mid-September to mid-October. In many parts of the country, it is dedicated to the worship of the goddesses Sarasvati, Lakshmi, and Durga. The ninth day of Navaratri is dedicated specifically to Sarasvati, who is the patron goddess of learning and music. In south India, all the musical instruments in the house, any writing implement, and selected educational textbooks are placed before the image of the goddess in order to receive blessings for the coming year. In some regions of India, it is a time when people acknowledge with respect the tools of their trade, whatever it may be. In some areas, vehicles such as cars and buses are decorated with garlands, and in recent years, typewriters and computers have been blessed with sacred powders and allowed to "rest" for a day before being used again.

The last day of Navaratri is dedicated to Lakshmi, the goddess of good fortune (see p. 28). On this day, after ritually writing the auspicious word "Shri" (a name of Lakshmi), people traditionally embark on ventures, open new business account books, and take up courses of learning. To mark the day, new prayers, pieces of music, and items of knowledge are learned, and great Hindu teachers are honored.

Dipavali ("Necklace of Lights") is probably the most widely observed Hindu festival. It falls on the new moon between mid-October and mid-November and is celebrated by decorating the home with lights, setting off fireworks, and wearing new clothes. Presents may be exchanged and festive meals are eaten. In south India, it is believed that Dipavali marks the day on which Krishna killed a demon, Narakasura, thus ensuring the triumph of light over darkness. In the north, it celebrates the return of the god Rama to Ayodhya and his coronation (see pp. 39–40). In Gujarat, it heralds the beginning of the New Year.

Pilgrims gather in Allahabad during the Kumbh Mela festival. These celebrations, held every 12 years, are the largest and most spectacular in the Hindu religious calendar.

In many parts of India, people rise before dawn on Dipavali for a ritual bath, because it is believed that on this day the holy waters of the Ganga river are present in all other water.

The many Hindu calendars and systems of reckoning time are all connected with the phases of the moon. These calendars are adjusted to the solar cycle regularly so that the festivals fall within the same season every year. The different parts of India celebrate New Year at different times of the year. In the state of Gujarat, for example, it falls a day after Dipavali. Elsewhere it may fall on the new moon closest to the spring equinox, or in the middle of April.

Sacred time can also be perceived as the time when one worships in a temple or at home. Temple worship forms a key element in Hindu religious life. In most temples, worship is traditionally not congregational, in the sense that people do not gather for communal worship at fixed times. There is no seating in the temple: devotees usually stand for a few minutes while they view the deity in its shrine. The closest thing to a religious congregation in Hinduism is when people gather together to listen to a religious teacher—although in most cases, this will take place in a public hall rather than in a temple—or to sing traditional religious songs at home and in other public places. This type of group singing is a common event at homes throughout India and in the diaspora.

Footwear is always left outside the temple precincts, a custom that symbolizes the worshipper's temporary abandonment of the dust and grime of worldly thoughts, preoccupations, and passions—a movement into sacred space and time. The simplest act of temple worship is to make the deity an offering of camphor, fruit, flowers, or coconut, all of which may often be bought at stalls outside the temple. In a small temple, the devotee may make the offering directly to the image of the deity, but in most places, the worshipper first hands the gift to a priest, who then presents it to the god or goddess. In many north Indian temples, ordinary worshippers may enter the innermost shrines, but in the south, access to these areas is restricted to priests and other initiates.

To the devotee, the most meaningful part of temple worship is the experience of seeing the deity (in the form of an image; see p. 24) and being in his or her presence. After the offering has been presented to the divine image, it is considered to have been "blessed" by the deity and to contain its "favor" (*prasada*). It is then returned to the worshipper. This simple act of viewing the deity, making an offering, and getting the sanctified offering back is the most popular of all Hindu votive rituals.

As in the temple, a deity that is worshipped in the home is considered to be a royal ruler and is treated accordingly. Members of the family may regularly light an oil lamp or incense sticks before the divine image, and make offerings of fruit or other foods. An altar, a shelf, a cabinet, or even an entire room in the house, may be set apart for devotional purposes and is sometimes filled with images of gods and goddesses.

When a group of devotees prays at home or in the temple, the ritual may end with an *arati*, or "waving of lamps." The attendant priest or one of the worshippers will light a piece of camphor in a plate, and sanctify it by waving it clockwise in front of the deity. The burning camphor is then shown to the worshippers, who briefly, but reverentially, place their hands over the flame and then touch their eyelids, as if to absorb the light of spiritual knowledge emanating from the supreme deity.

Single and married women—but not widows— frequently perform special votive observances called *vrata*. Many of these rituals are domestic in nature and observed for the welfare of the husband, the extended family, or the community. Sanskrit manuals claim that these rites enable a woman to attain liberation from the cycle of birth and death, but most women perform them simply for happiness in the home. After prayers to a domestic deity, women may eat together and distribute auspicious substances, such as bananas, coconuts, turmeric, and *kum kum* (a red powder that is daubed on the forehead). A *vrata* may last from a few minutes to five days, with periods of fasting alternating with communal meals.

In northern India, many women's rites focus on the welfare of male relatives. For example, in the lunar month from mid-October to mid-November, women undertake two fasts on the fourth and eighth days of the waning moon for the benefit of their husbands and sons. In much of south India, spiritually empowering women's rituals take place in the lunar month from mid-July to mid-August. *Brahmin* women pray to the goddess Lakshmi for domestic well-being. Non-*brahmin* women may take special pots of water and milk to temples of a local goddess as offerings on behalf of their family, or they may cook rice and milk dishes to distribute. At the temples of the powerful regional goddess Draupadi Amman (a principal character in the *Mahabharata* epic), women and men alike may enter a trance and walk over hot coals in a ceremony euphemistically called "walking on flowers."

The Hindu tradition, like other religions, possesses numerous rituals marking an individual's transition from one stage of life to another. In some sacred texts, the life-cycle sacraments begin with the birth of a child, while in others they begin with marriage, for it is then that the life of a person is believed truly to begin. While some life-cycle rites are pan-Hindu, many are purely local celebrations, particularly women's rituals.

Like all significant Hindu sacraments, rites of passage must take place in the presence of a sacred fire. The importance of fire (Sanskrit: *agni*) can be traced as far back as the Vedic period. Early Vedic rituals (see p. 13) were performed around an altar of fire, and fire was thought of as the master of the house. Offerings are made to the sacred fire during prenatal rites, when a child is one year old, during weddings—indeed the marriage ceremony is valid only if the couple take their vows before a fire, which is deemed to be the cosmic witness to the sacrament—and when a man reaches the ages of sixty and eighty. Finally, when a person dies, his or her body is offered up to the flames. Annual rites to commemorate one's ancestors are also performed before a fire.

Auspicious times are chosen for the conduct of all life-cycle sacraments. These times are in accordance with a person's horoscope, which is cast at birth. Almanacs also detail the auspicious dates in a calendar. These traditional almanacs are consulted regularly for scheduling all important events in one's life, including rites of passage, entering a new home, embarking on an important trip, or starting a new venture. It is believed that astrologically propitious moments maximize the possibilities of success.

The Ages of the Universe

" When a thousand eons are over there is a drought for many years; there are few resources and creatures starve to death . . . fires of destruction overcome this earth . . . awesome clouds rise high. At the end of time, human beings will be uncivilized and eat any flesh . . . When the end of this age of time is drawing near, it will not rain, crops will not grow . . . "

Mahabharata, translated by Vasudha Narayanan.

Commentary

While Hindus choose astrologically propitious times in which to perform their various rituals, the units of time that are spoken of in Hindu texts concerning the creation and destruction of the universe are astronomical.

One day in the life of the minor creator god Brahma lasts 4,320 million earthly years. There are distinctions between earthly years and the years of the gods, which are far longer. The total of 360 such days and 360 nights makes one Brahmic year, and Brahma lives for 100 years. This cycle is therefore 311,040,000 million years.

The end of each cycle of creation is marked by cataclysmic events, such as those described in the passage from the *Mahabharata*, above. After this period, the entire cosmos is drawn into the body of Vishnu and remains there until another Brahma has evolved.

The units of time are further subdivided into specific cycles (*yuga*s, or world ages). The first world age, the golden age, lasts for 1,728,000 earth years. During this time, *dharma*, or righteousness, reigns but thereafter a gradual deterioration of morality, righteousness, and well-being takes place. When we come to the fourth, last, and most degenerate age in the cycle (the *kali yuga*, the present age in which we live), *dharma* has almost completely disappeared. This age lasts for 432,000 earth years and, according to traditional Hindu reckoning, began around 3102 BCE.

At the end of the *kali yuga*—obviously, still a long time off—there will be no righteousness, no virtue, no trace of justice. When the world ends, seven scorching suns will dry up the oceans; after the drought there will be a deluge; there will be wondrously shaped clouds, torrential rains will fall and, eventually, the cosmos will be absorbed into Vishnu. While, according to many Hindu systems of thought, it is possible for a human being to end his or her cycle of birth and death and gain liberation, the cycles of creation and destruction of the universe are independent of the human being's attaining *moksha* or liberation.

CHAPTER EIGHT

DEATH AND THE AFTERLIFE

Most Hindus believe in the immortality of the soul and in reincarnation. There is also popular belief in ghosts and spirits, including those that may possess people. A person's death is followed by rebirth, and the cycle of birth and death continues until one attains liberation (*moksha*). Rebirth is perceived as suffering, and the happiness one has on earth is said to be temporary. Liberation is conceptualized in several ways, including: as ineffable and beyond words; as a loving union with the supreme being; as losing one's consciousness in the supreme being; and as being in the heavenly abode of Vishnu, called Vaikuntha. Many texts and temple sculptures (including Angkor Wat in Cambodia) present notions of a temporary paradise called *svarga*, accounts of Vaikuntha, as well as several kinds of hell.

LEFT: Mount Kailas in Tibet, the abode of the Hindu god Shiva. Emancipated souls are believed to enter this heavenly paradise after death. Some claim that, when viewed from a particular angle, the ice-covered dome of Kailas resembles a human skull.

One distinctive characteristic of the religions that began in the Indian subcontinent is the belief in *karma*, an idea first occurring around the seventh century BCE. *Karma* literally means "action," especially ritual action, but after the compilation of the *Upanishad*s (ca. 600 BCE; see p. 38), it came to mean the concept of rewards and punishments attached to various acts.

Underlying the theory of *karma* is the idea of the immortality of the soul. Although the early *Veda*s contain a nebulous notion of an afterlife, by the time of the *Upanishad*s it was claimed that the human soul existed forever, and that after death it underwent rebirth or reincarnation (*samsara*). The "law of *karma*" thus refers to a system of cause and effect that may span several lifetimes. It dictates that human beings gain merit (*punya*) or demerit (*papa*) from every action they perform. Good deeds and bad deeds do not simply cancel each other out; one has to experience the fruits of all actions in the course of many lives. The balance of *punya* and *papa* acquired in one lifetime determines the nature and quality of one's next existence.

Liberation (*moksha*) from this pattern, according to the *Upanishad*s, comes from a supreme, experiential wisdom. In acquiring this transforming knowledge, one has a profound insight into one's own immortality (*amrta*), from which point the soul ceases to possess the ability to be reborn. Rebirth and its connection with *karma* (notions central to the later Hindu tradition) are thus clearly articulated in the *Upanishad*s, as is the ultimate goal of every human being—liberation from the unending cycle of birth and death and from the attendant human suffering implied by experiencing multiple lifetimes (see pp. 60–61).

Since the time of the *Upanishad*s, Hindus have taken the notions of *karma* and immortality for granted. However, the various Hindu traditions differ on what happens to the soul when it is ultimately liberated from the cycle of life and death. For some, the soul experiences a joyous devotional relationship with the supreme being. Others speak of an identification with the supreme being.

A number of writings describe the soul's journey after death. Although reincarnation and liberation are the most frequently discussed aspects of the afterlife in Hinduism, the *Purana*s (see p. 39 and p. 42) talk of many kinds of heaven and hell. In the Hindu tradition, a soul's sojourn in a hell or paradise is generally seen as being temporary. A soul is reborn in such a region if it has accumulated certain kinds of good or bad *karma*; but once this *karma* is exhausted, the soul moves on into a different form of existence.

*The flower-bedecked funeral procession of Indira Gandhi
(Prime Minister of India, 1966–1977 and 1980–1984)
in Delhi, following her assassination in November 1984.
The ceremony culminated with her cremation on a pyre.*

According to some texts, a soul that has attained
emancipation from the cycle of life, death, and rebirth
crosses a river called Viraja ("Without Passion") and
enters a heavenly paradise, either Vaikuntha (the abode
of Vishnu) or Kailasa (the mountain abode of Shiva
on the borders of India and Tibet). Devotees of these
gods imagine their heavenly dwellings as places filled

with other devotees singing his praises. Vaikuntha is sometimes described as a place filled with light.

As far as unemancipated souls are concerned, none of the Hindu sacred texts discuss the details of what happens immediately after death or even between lifetimes. While it is clear that one's *karma* accumulated from previous lifetimes is believed to influence what sort of life will follow, the holy books offer no theories about how long it takes before a soul is reincarnated. Nor is there any discussion or explanation of why people do not remember their past lives, although in popular belief it is claimed that many people do indeed recall small pieces of previous existences. Only the truly evolved souls, the great spiritual leaders and teachers, are said to remember all their past lives.

Many texts speak of the repellent nature of this life and urge human beings to seek everlasting "real" life through the liberation of the soul. Others, however, state that by glorifying God on earth one can achieve the experience of heaven in one's lifetime. To this end, sacred pilgrimage centers offer a break from the daily rhythms of earthly existence and the opportunity for divine revelation. Some Hindus consider that a life lived in praise of the divine is a joyful experience that is not merely an imitation of a state of liberation, but that state itself.

Salvation and Liberation

&& Words go but return without reaching it; the mind does not grasp it. One who knows the bliss of [knowing] *brahman* is not afraid.

[A person who is enlightened] does not worry: 'why did I not do the right thing?' 'Why did I do what is wrong?' A person who knows is freed . . . **&&**

Taittiriya Upanishad, 2.9.1, translated by Vasudha Narayanan.

&& Vishnu/Krishna says:

'Even if various kinds of liberation are offered to [my devotees]—

    living in the same place as I do,

    equality in wealth, power, and glory

    being near me,

    having a form like mine

    and even union with the supreme,

they will still choose only to serve me. **&&**

Bhagavata Purana, III. 29.13, translated by Vasudha Narayanan.

Commentary

Hindu texts have conceptualized the final goal of human beings with notions of heaven and hell and as being completely beyond description. The *Upanishad*s speak about *brahman* (the supreme being), *karma*, and the afterlife. Since that time, Hindu traditions have thought of the final goal of all beings as liberation. As the first passage suggests, this superlative state involves having the bliss of *brahman* but is otherwise indescribable.

All beings are said to be born only to die again. Since all actions incur *karma*, one is born to experience the results of one's actions from lives past. One is trapped in this cycle until one's *karma* ends and one's soul is liberated. While the *Upanishad*s speak of the final state as ineffable, in texts and traditions of devotion, serving the deity—envisaged as Vishnu, Shiva, or the Goddess—is considered to be the highest goal.

In the second passage, taken from the *Bhagavata Purana*, Krishna lists several kinds of states in liberation, all of which are conceptualized in an anthropomorphic way. In some, the emancipated soul lives in the same place as Krishna, others have (almost) equal glory, some are near him and others have a form like his. Union with him is also possible, but, he says, the true devotee always seeks to serve Krishna. Occasionally, some texts speak about various kinds of hell. That these were active in the imaginations of Hindus is seen from their depictions in sculptures, as on the entire south corridor of the famous Vishnu temple at Angkor Wat in Cambodia.

CHAPTER NINE

SOCIETY AND RELIGION

Hinduism is a distinctly life-affirming religion and Hindu *dharma* speaks about the individual's obligations to the community. Hindu society is marked by different hierarchies that include caste, gender, age, and piety, and by practices that involve meditation, devotional singing, and dietary control. Although the textual sources focus on four major classes (priestly or *brahmin*; royalty and warrior; merchant and producer; and "servant") there are actually thousands of castes in Hinduism and the other religions of India.

The position of women in Hinduism has been complex; they have been both empowered and subjugated by the tradition. Powerful women poets, patrons, and philosophers have lived alongside those who have been repressed by male-dominated norms and customs.

LEFT: A Hindu bride at her marriage ceremony. In order to ensure a harmonious union, a Hindu marriage takes place only after a period of prolonged matchmaking— this can often include consideration of caste, birthplace, and horoscopes.

Until recently, the word "Hindu" has seldom been used as a signifier of identity in India. A person's position in society has depended much more intimately on his or her social "class" (*varna*), birth group (*jati*), religious sectarian community, and philosophical allegiance.

While texts speak of four major *varna*s, there are hundreds of *jati*s. The earliest mention of distinct social classes within Indian society occurs in the *Veda*s. In discussing a cosmic sacrifice, in which the various elements of the universe arise from the body of a primordial cosmic man, the *Rig Veda* declares: "From his mouth came the priestly class, from his arms, the rulers. The producers came from his legs; from his feet came the servant class" (*Rig Veda* 10.90). Although some have seen these verses as the origin of what eventually came to be called the "caste system" (Portuguese *casta*, "social division"), it is probable that the stratification of Indian society had begun long before the composition of the text.

These initial four broad *varna*s were the priests (*brahmins*), the rulers and warriors (*kshatriya*s), the merchants and producers (*vaishya*s), and the servants (*shudra*s). The latter two, at least, were always broad groupings, and while in time it came to be expected that members of all classes would, in theory, pursue the vocation associated with their particular group, it is likely that this prescription was not far-reaching. Today, while some *jati*s can be fitted loosely into the ancient fourfold division, hundreds more have an ambiguous relation to it.

Members of the priestly, warrior, and merchant groups were sometimes known as the "upper" castes, and their male members were known as the "twice born" because of their traditional initiation ritual of spiritual rebirth called *upanayana*. Through this, they become invested with a "sacred thread" that grants them the power to study the *Veda*s.

By the first centuries of the Common Era, many treatises on righteousness, moral duty, and law, known as *dharmashastra*s, were composed. The *dharmashastra*s outline the duties and privileges of the four main *varna*s (classes) of society. The *brahmin* (priestly) class retained sole authority to teach and learn the *Veda*s. Many of the *brahmin*s were teachers, priests, and ritual specialists.

The former kings and princes of India belonged to the *kshatriya* ("royal," or "warrior") class that traditionally held the reins of secular power. Many *kshatriya*s traced their ancestry back to primeval divine progenitors of humanity—in Hinduism, to this day, claimed lines of descent are highly important—and later Hindu rituals explicitly emphasized their direct connection with divine beings.

The mercantile class (*vaishya*s) were in charge of trade, commerce, and farming, and were thus potential possessors of great wealth and economic power. *Shudra*s (servants) are not allowed to accumulate wealth, even if they are able to do so. The law texts state that the duty of a *shudra* is to serve the other classes.

The caste system was—and is—far more complex and flexible than the behavior the *dharmashastra*s advocated, and historical evidence suggests that their prescriptions were probably not taken too seriously by many classes of society and apparently not followed at all in many areas. For instance, the *jati* called Vellalas were technically a *shudra* caste, but in practice they were wealthy landowners who wielded considerable economic and political power in the south. The *dharmashastra* prohibitions seem to have had no effect on their fortunes.

Eventually, various groups of "outcastes" emerged who were not covered by the law codes. These arose either from mixed marriages or more often from association with professions that were deemed inferior.

While various texts and practices do clearly imply the hierarchy of the castes, some Hindus have interpreted the traditional system as an equal division of labor, with each major group being responsible for a particular area of activity essential to society.

It has been widely debated whether caste originally depended on birth or simply on a person's qualifications. The Sanskrit word *jati* implies the former, but some discussions in the epic *Mahabharata* suggest that the situation may once have been less clear-cut (see pp. 104–105). This and other texts think of caste as incumbent on one's propensities. Several devotional movements

A brahmin priest in Bengal is shown blessing an account book. Brahmins (see pp. 98–99) traditionally represented the intelligentsia, providing teachers and performing religious sacraments. In the Hindu caste system they are considered the highest of the four social classes.

in India have also challenged the social validity of caste and have advocated hierarchies that are based on faith alone.

To this day, people continue regularly to identify themselves by their *jati*, and the entire Indian caste system is such a strong social force that non-Hindu communities such as the Christians, Jains, and Sikhs have absorbed parts of it. For example, Nadar Christians in the south of India will only consider marrying people of the same heritage.

Sectarian, philosophical, and regional allegiances cut across caste lines and provide a different basis for social identification. Hindu sects are determined by the god they worship—Vaishnavas are devotees of Vishnu, Shaivas of Shiva, and so on. Philosophical communities— followers of such great thinkers as Shankara (eighth century CE), Ramanuja (eleventh century CE), and Chaitanya (sixteenth century CE)—also form distinct groups in many parts of India. Regional identity is important, too. As the thousands of matrimonial advertisements in weekly newspapers and the Internet suggest, Hindus tend to marry partners who not only come from the same *jati*, sectarian community, philosophical group, and geographical area, but also who possess compatible horoscopes.

On the whole, Hindu literature has expressed

paradoxical views on the role and position of women. The Laws of Manu, written at the beginning of the Common Era (see p. 66), implies that contemporary women were accorded a low status.

Underlying many of the attitudes expressed by male religious writers is the concept of "auspiciousness." Essentially, a person or thing is auspicious if it promotes the three goals of *dharma* (duty), *artha* (prosperity), and *kama* (sensual pleasure). Thus, in the *dharmashastra*s, and in Hindu practice to this day, it is auspicious for a woman to be married and thus be a full partner in *dharma*, *artha*, and *kama*.

However, while Manu may have been quoted with enthusiasm by male writers on Hindu law—whose works have informed many Western notions of Indian womanhood—many Hindu women have always enjoyed, as they do today, a degree of religious and financial independence and have made an important and lasting contribution to the culture of their homeland. Even in the Vedic age, women composed hymns and took part in philosophical debates. After the eighth century CE, there were women poets, temple patrons, philosophers, religious commentators, and writers of scholarly works—such women were respected, honored, and, in some cases, even venerated.

Becoming a *Brahmin*

❝ Nahusha asked Yudhishthira:

'Who can be said to be a *brahmin*, O King?'

Yudhishthira replied:

'O lord of Serpents! The one who is truthful,

is generous, is patient, is virtuous, has empathy,

is tranquil, and has compassion—such a person

is a *brahmin*.' **❞**

Mahabharata Vana Parva , 177.15, translated by Vasudha Narayanan.

Commentary

As anyone reading the matrimonial advertisements in Indian newspapers or on the Internet can immediately detect, caste identity is very important for the Hindu community. Along with age, economic status, gender, and issues surrounding piety and practice, caste is one of the many factors that have determined social hierarchies in India for thousands of years.

But the concept of caste is complex. While it is almost always understood in Indian society to be incumbent on birth and birth groups, there have been many contexts in which alternative interpretations have been possible, or in which the conventional hierarchal structures have been inverted.

In the passage quoted opposite, from the *Mahabharata* ("Great Epic of India" or, alternatively, "Great Sons of Bharata"; see pp. 39–41), a serpent king interrogates Yudhishthira, the wise Pandava brother, as to who can be said to be a *brahmin*. The question comes up again later in the epic when a Yaksha, a semi-divine entity, queries Yudhishthira on the same issue: ". . . is a *brahmin* born or can one recognize a *brahmin* by one's propensity?" Yudhishthira's answer seems to suggest the latter, that *brahmin*-hood is determined by "propensity," or behavior. However, this issue has given rise to considerable speculation and debate in Hindu practice. The many virtues spoken of by Yudhishthira as markers of *brahmin*-hood have ordinarily been considered to be signifiers of *sanatana dharma*, or the eternal faith of the Hindus in the many Hindu texts.

At various moments in the history of Hinduism, a person of "low" caste, or sometimes even one who is beyond the pale of the caste system, is considered to be a paradigmatic devotee, thus suggesting a social revolution. But while the superiority of devotees is recognized, without heeding caste, the divisions have, on the whole, been dominant—not just in Hinduism, but also in other religions of the sub-continent, including Christianity, Jainism, and Sikhism.

GLOSSARY

adharma Evil; immorality; disorder; unrighteousness.
artha Wealth, success; one of the four aims or *purusartha*s of life.
avatar The descent of a god in bodily form.
Bhagavad Gita "Song of the Lord" (within the *Mahabharata*).
Brahma The creator god.
brahman The universal soul that is present in all things.
brahmin The highest of the four classes; the priestly class (also written as *brahmana*).
dharma Responsibility; ethics; law; moral and cosmic order. The principle of order that governs the universe and individual lives.
kama Love; pleasure; one of the four aims of human life.
karma Sanskrit, "action." The balance of merit and demerit accumulated by an individual, which determines the nature of one's next reincarnation.
Mahabharata Great martial epic of the Hindus that provides guidance on moral living.
moksha Release from ignorance and the cycle of rebirths, often characterized as the union of an individual with the divine.
Puranas Sacred collection of legends and ritual practice.
*purusartha*s The four aims of human life, namely, *dharma, artha, kama* and *moksha.*
Ramayana A Hindu epic in which Rama, *avatar* of Vishnu, defeats the demon Ravana and is reunited with his lover Sita.
shakti Divine energy, characterized as feminine and personified by the Goddess.
smriti Remembering; refers to those authoritative religious texts that are popularly preserved in the Hindu memory; they are composed by humans, although divinely inspired.
Upanishads Mystical texts of speculative philosophy.
*Veda*s Sanskrit texts that reveal *veda* or sacred knowledge, compiled (ca. 750–600 BCE).
Vishnu Sustainer of the universe whose *avatar*s descend from time to time to re-establish order in the world of humans
yuga An era of the world.

FOR MORE INFORMATION

Cambridge University Hindu Cultural Society
University of Cambridge
Trinity Lane
Cambridge CB2 1TN
England
Web site: http://www.cuhcs.org.uk
University organization that works to educate people in Hindu philosophy and provide a support network for Hindu students.

Hindu American Foundation
5268G Nicholson Lane #164

Kensington, MD 20895
(301) 770-7835
Web site: http://www.hinduamericanfoundation.org/index.php
Advocacy group that provides a support base for Hindu Americans by protecting their religious rights and promoting understanding and tolerance.

Hindu Heritage Endowment
107 Kaholalele Road
Kapaa, HI 96746
(808) 822-3012
Web site: http://www.hheonline.org
A public charitable trust that was created to support and maintain Hindu projects and institutions all over the world.

Hindu Society of Calgary
2225 24th Avenue, NE
Calgary, Alberta T2E 8M2
Canada
(403) 291-2551
Web site: http://www.calgarymandir.com
Society that provides religious, cultural, and social services in Calgary and the surrounding area.

Web Sites
Due to the changing nature of Internet links, Rosen Publishing has developed an online list of Web sites related to the subject of this book. This site is updated regularly. Please use this link to access the list:

http://www.rosenlinks.com/rel/hind

FOR FURTHER READING

Bhaskarananda, Swami. *The Essentials of Hinduism: A Comprehensive Overview of the World's Oldest Religion.* Seattle, WA: Viveka Press, 2002.
Doniger, Wendy. *The Hindus: An Alternative History.* New York, NY: Penguin, 2009.
Easwaran, Eknath. *The Bhagavad Gita.* Tomales, CA: Nilgiri Press, 2007.
Glucklich, Ariel. *The Strides of Vishnu: Hindu Culture in Historical Perspective.* New York, NY: Oxford University Press, 2008.
Johnsen, Linda. *The Complete Idiot's Guide to Hinduism.* New York, NY: Alpha Books, 2001.
Kapur, Kamla K. *Ganesha Goes to Lunch: Classics from Mystic India.* San Rafael, CA: Mandala, 2007.
Klostermaier, Klaus K. *Hinduism: A Beginner's Guide.* Oxford, England: Oneworld Publications, 2008.

Lasater, Judith Hanson. *A Year of Living Your Yoga: Daily Practices to Shape Your Life*. Berkeley, CA: Rodmell Press, 2006.

Mann, Gurinder, Paul Numrich, and Raymond Williams. *Buddhists, Hindus, and Sikhs in America: A Short History*. New York, NY: Oxford University Press, 2007.

Sharma, Arvind. *A Guide to Hindu Spirituality*. Bloomington, IN: World Wisdom, 2006.

GENERAL BIBLIOGRAPHY

Baird, Robert D. (ed.) *Religion and Law in Independent India*. New Delhi, India: Manohar, 1993.

Basham, Arthur L. *The Wonder That Was India: A Survey of the History and Culture of the Indian Sub-continent Before the Coming of the Muslims*. 3rd ed. London, England: Sidgwick and Jackson, 1967.

Danielou, A. *Hindu Polytheism*. New York, NY: Bollingen Foundation, 1964.

Doniger, Wendy, and Brin Smith. (trans.) *The Laws of Manu*. Harmondsworth, England: Penguin, 1991.

Eck, Diana L. *Darsan: Seeing the Divine Image in India*. Chambersburg, PA: Anima, 1981.

Erndl, Kathleen M. *Victory to the Mother*. New York, NY: Oxford University Press, 1993.

Gandhi, Mahatma. *An Autobiography: The Story of My Experiments with Truth*. Ahmadabad, India: Navjivan Publications, 1959.

Hart, George. *Poets of the Tamil Anthologies: Ancient Poems of Love and War*. Princeton, NJ: Princeton University Press, 1979.

Hawley, John S., and Donna M. Wulff. (eds.) *Devi: Goddesses of India*. Berkeley, CA: University of California Press, 1996.

Hawley, John S., and Mark Juergensmeyer. *Songs of the Saints of India*. New York, NY: Oxford University Press, 1988.

Hiriyanna, Mysore. *The Essentials of Indian Philosophy*. London, England: Allen and Unwin, 1960.

Kane, P.V. *History of Dharmasastra*. 5 vols. Poona, India: Bhandarkar Oriental Research Institute, 1953–1974.

Leslie, Julia. (ed.) *Roles and Rituals for Hindu Women*. Rutherford, NJ: Fairleigh Dickinson University Press, 1991.

Miller, Barbara Stoler. (trans.) *The Bhagavad Gita: Krishna's Counsel in Time of War*. New York, NY: Columbia University Press, 1986.

Narayan, R.K. *The Ramayana*. New York, NY: Viking, 1972.

Narayan, R.K. *The Mahabharata*. New York, NY: Viking, 1978.

Narayanan, Vasudha. *The Vernacular Veda: Revelation, Recitation and Ritual*. Columbia, SC: University of South Carolina Press, 1994.

O'Flaherty, W.D. *Hindu Myths: A Sourcebook*. Baltimore, MD: Penguin, 1975.

Olivelle, Patrick. (trans.) *The Upanisads*. New York, NY: Oxford University Press, 1996.

Pandey, Raj Bali. *Hindu Samskaras: Socio-religious Studies of the Hindu Sacraments*. Delhi, India: Motilal Banarsidass, 1982.

Peterson, Indira Viswanathan. *Poems to Siva: The Hymns of the Tamil Saints*. Princeton, NJ: Princeton University Press, 1990.

Singer, Milton B. *Krishna: Myths, Rites, and Attitudes*. Honolulu, HI: East-West Center Press, 1966.

Waghorne Joanne P., Norman Cutler, and Vasudha Narayanan. *Gods of Flesh, Gods of Stone: The Embodiment of Divinity in India.* Chambersburg, PA: Anima, 1985.

Young, Katherine. "Hinduism" in *Women in World Religions.* (ed. Arvind Sharma). Albany, NY: State University of NY Press, 1987.

INDEX

ABOUT THE AUTHOR

Vasudha Narayanan is Robin and Jean Gibson Professor of Liberal Arts and Sciences and Professor in the Department of Religion at the University of Florida. She is also president of the Society of Hindu-Christian Studies. She has lectured widely, and her publications include *The Vernacular Veda: Revelation, Recitation, and Ritual* and *The Way and the Goal: Expressions of Devotion in the Early Sri Vaisnava Tradition.*

ACKNOWLEDGMENTS AND PICTURE CREDITS

All the text extracts have been translated by the author.

The publisher would like to thank the following people, museums, and photographic libraries for permission to reproduce their material. Every care has been taken to trace copyright holders. However, if we have omitted anyone we apologize, and will, if informed, make corrections in any future edition.

Cover, pp. 1, 3 (left), cover, back cover (background) © www.istockphoto.com/Jeremy Edwards; cover, pp. 1, 3 (top center) © www.istockphoto.com/x-drew; cover, pp. 1, 3 (right) © www.istockphoto.com/Shannon Varis; cover, p. 1 (top left) © www.istockphoto.com/Rick Donovan; cover, p. 1 (top right) © www.istockphoto.com/Anantha Vardhan; cover (bottom) © www.istockphoto.com/dndavis.

Page 2 Corbis/Dallas and John Heaton; **8** Robert Harding, London/ Richard Ashworth; **10** Robert Harding, London/JHC Wilson; **18** Robert Harding, London/ Gavin Hellier; **22** Corbis/ Kelly-Mooney Photography; **27** Robert Harding, London/Richard Ashworth; **36** Corbis/ Barnabas Bosshart; **40** Corbis/ Burstein Collection; **48** Corbis/ SYGMA/Bossu Regis; **53** Corbis/ Chris Lisle; **56** Corbis/Brian A. Vikander; **60** AKG images/ British Library; **64** Corbis/Adam Woolfitt; **69** Corbis/David Samuel Robbins; **76** Corbis/ Amit Bhargava; **80** Magnum Photos, London/Alex Majoli; **88** Corbis/Galen Rowell; **92** Corbis/ David Turnley; **96** Magnum Photos, London/Ian Berry; **101** Robert Harding, London/Duncan Maxwell.